THE GREAT GUNS OF HMS VICTORY

by
Michael D. Prior

PUBLISHED BY CHAIN-SHOT BOOKS

136 Hazleton Way, Waterlooville, PO8 9DP
United Kingdom

mdp@chainshotbooks.co.uk

First Edition 1985

Re-printed 2012

Second Edition 2014

Third Edition 2015

Copyright Michael D Prior 2014

Acknowledgements

My thanks are due to Lieutenant Commander W.E.Pearce MVO RN
Retd. One time Commanding Officer of HMS VICTORY for his help
in producing this book and to Robert Wright for his painstaking
efforts, skill and research in providing the excellent illustrations.

Thanks are also due to John Loader, Nick Collister and Sue
Washington for their help in putting together a much needed
publication to satisfy the requirements of students of naval gunnery.

ISBN Number: 978 0 9928411 1 9

Introduction

This booklet was written to satisfy the curiosity of members of the General Public who visit HMS VICTORY in The Portsmouth Heritage Dockyard. It explains What, How, When and Why the British Royal Navy was the supreme naval force in the 17th, 18th and 19th Centuries.

The author spent many hours in research and is grateful for the assistance of experts in the field of Art and Naval history from the National Maritime Museum (Greenwich), The "Victory" Museum in Portsmouth Heritage Dockyard and the co-operation of the Late Dr. Colin White, Director of the "Victory" Museum in the Heritage Dockyard.

As HMS VICTORY received a number of changes of armaments during her sea service, this booklet is therefore an amalgam of these changes.

Contents

PREFACE

The first HMS VICTORY was originally a merchant ship named CHRISTOPHER and launched in 1559. She was purchased for the Navy in 1561 and renamed VICTORY. Rebuilt in 1586 she carried the flag of Sir John Hawkins at the Battle of the Armada (1588). When rebuilt she weighed 800 tons, carried 34 guns, 300 mariners, 34 gunners and 400 soldiers.

The second HMS VICTORY was launched in 1620. Designed by Phineas Pett she was of 873 tons and carried 42 guns. Rebuilt in 1665 and increased in size to 1029 tons she eventually carried 82 guns. This VICTORY took part in the Dutch wars and her battle honours from 1652-1673 are Dover, Gabbard, Scheveingen, Orfordness, Solebay, Schooneveld and Texel.

The third HMS VICTORY was launched in 1675 as the ROYAL JAMES and renamed in 1691. Of 1486 tons she carried 100 guns and 754 men. The battle honour for this ship is Barfleur in 1692.

The fourth HMS VICTORY was built at Portsmouth and launched in 1737. She weighed 1920 tons and carried 110 guns and 900 men. She was lost in the Channel with all hands in 1744.

The fifth and last HMS VICTORY was laid down in the Single Dock in Chatham in 1759 and launched in 1765.

After completing Sea Trials she was placed in Ordinary and remained there until May 1778 when Admiral Keppel hoisted his flag in her. For the next 44 years she took part in a number of engagements and battles including her finest hour at the Battle of Trafalgar in 1805. Laid up in Portsmouth in 1812 she remained at her berth for 110 years and carried the flags of successive Admirals commanding Portsmouth. In 1922 her removal to the No 2 Dock in Portsmouth was undertaken at the behest of the Society for Nautical Research and restoration to the appearance she held in 1805 was started. This restoration was completed in 1928 and the ship then re-opened to the public. Her battle honours are 1781 Ushant, 1797 St Vincent and of course 1805 Trafalgar.

HMS Victory

THE ROYAL CYPHER OF KING GEORGE III

Rubbing taken from original Trafalgar Cannon.

THE ARMAMENT

During her life HMS VICTORY has had many changes in her armament. The following list shows the dates of the changes:

1765   Original
- 30 x 42 Pdrs   Lower Gun Deck
- 28 x 24 Pdrs   Middle Gun Deck
- 30 x 12 Pdrs   Upper Gun Deck
- 10 x 6 Pdrs   Quarterdeck
- 2 x 6 Pdrs   Fo'csle

1778   30 x 42 Pdrs removed and replaced by same number of 32 Pdr guns

1780   2 x 24 Pdr Carronades and 6 x 18 Pdr Carronades fitted on Poop

1783   All 6 Pdrs removed and replaced by 12 Pdr guns

1793   Poop guns removed and never replaced

1803   42 Pdr guns again replaced by 32 Pdrs. The 42 Pdr guns were brought back to the ship some time after Admiral Keppel left in 1780

In the period 1759-1774 a new type of gun was being manufactured by the Carron Company of Falkirk, Scotland. These guns were made in various sizes from 12 to 68 Pdrs and there is even mention of 130 Pdrs. Two of the largest size - 68 Pdrs - were supplied to HMS VICTORY in 1805 so that when she joined the Fleet off Cadiz, before the Battle of Trafalger, her armament was the most modern available. All her guns were made of iron and all but two were mounted on wooden carriages. The exceptions were the two carronades which were mounted on swivelling slide mountings. The total armament was; 104 guns consisting of

- 30 x 32 Pdrs   Lower Gun Deck
- 28 x 24 Pdrs   Middle Gun Deck
- 30 x 12 Pdrs   Upper Gun Deck
- 2 x 68 Pdrs   Carronades Fo'csle
- 2 x 12 Pdrs   Fo'csle
- 12 x 12 Pdrs   Quarterdeck

	WEIGHT OF GUNS			MAX RANGE	
32	65cwt	7280 pounds	3276 kilos	2640 yds	2402 mtrs
24	58cwt	6496 pounds	2923 kilos	1760 yds	1603 mtrs
12L	40.1cwt	4491 pounds	2021 kilos	1320 yds	1201 mtrs
12M	37.8cwt	4234 pounds	1905 kilos	1300 yds	1183 mtrs
12S	36.6cwt	4099 pounds	1845 kilos	1280 yds	1147 mtrs

NAPOLEONIC GUNS

There are eleven examples of Napoleonic guns on board. 8 X 32 Pdrs on the Lower Gun Deck and 3 X 24 Pdrs on the Middle Gun Deck. These guns are of the pattern devised by Sir Thomas Blomefield, Inspector General of Ordnance, and cast in the late - 1700s. The remainder of the guns are manufactured from either teak or fibreglass. The Royal Cypher of George III is clearly visible on all guns.

When guns were supplied to a ship a record was made of the manufacturers name and the number that he gave to the gun. The iron guns on display are marked on the trunnion with either W.Co or H.Co. The former stands for Walker and Company of Rotherham, Yorkshire and the latter stands for J Henckell and Company of London.

In order that economies could be made, ships in refit would land a large percentage of the armament to be used by others. The records which show which guns HMS VICTORY received have been lost at both the factory and the Admiralty due to fires and bomb damage. It is not possible therefore, to categorically state that the guns now fitted were in the ship at the Battle of Trafalgar, but it is certain that they are of that period.

Note
The guns on the dockside are short barrelled 32 Pdrs cast during the reign of George III but not issued until 1847. These guns used to be the saluting battery when HMS VICTORY was moored in the harbour and were removed to the dockside in 1922. It was these guns which fired the salute to the young Queen Victoria when she made her way to London for her Coronation.

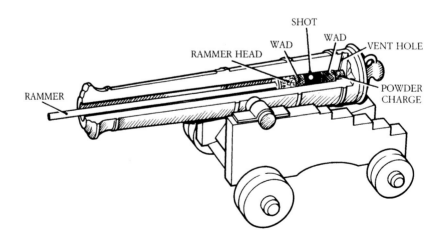

CONSTRUCTION OF CARRIAGES

Construction of gun carriages for HMS VICTORY followed the same method used for many years. Some of the gun carriages on display are very old and made of oak, others were made of teak in the period 1922-28. A carriage recovered from the wreck of the ROYAL GEORGE sunk off Portsmouth in 1782 is on view in the Royal Naval Museum and this shows the same method of construction.

All the fittings on the gun carriage are of wrought iron. The wheels, proper name is trucks, on which the carriage roll, are made of cross-grained curly English elm. Each truck is made of two pieces of wood assembled so that the grain of one piece runs at right angles to the other. The fastenings consist of 6 iron clench bolts and the trucks are easily removed from their axles in the event of damage. The lower gun deck, known to be the original timber from 1759, shows very little signs of wear and this is believed to be the result of using wooden wheels.

The gun carriages in HMS VICTORY are painted yellow in accordance with a directive issued by the Admiralty Board in 1791.

Lord Nelson

Originally the gun carriages and the inside of the ship were painted red but this directive altered the specifications and now only the gun port lids are painted red. The weight of a 32 pounder carriage is approximately 1680 lbs

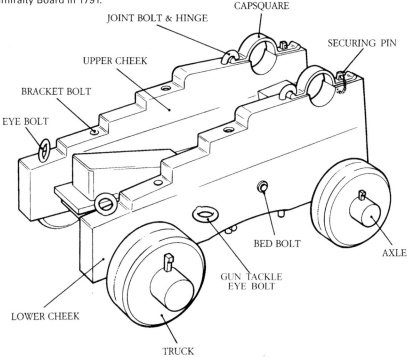

9

CONSTRUCTION OF CANNON

Cannon for the Navy were initially constructed of strips or bars of blacksmith made wrought iron bound with circlets of iron. These guns were tied to a wooden frame loaded with powder and fired by a slow match. Further developments included a primitive form of breech loading and the use of brass cannons. The French, Dutch and Germans produced the best brass or bronze cannons at this time and these were imported to arm the Fleet.

The advent of the Industrial Revolution led to the use of cast iron and wrought iron in gun manufacture. Many iron foundries were created throughout the country some small and some large. With only a few exceptions all the cannon remaining in HMS VICTORY and on the dockside are the work of Walkers and Company of Rotherham in Yorkshire. This thriving company continued in business for many years as gun founders. One major problem associated with the casting of cannon was to ensure that the metal of the casting contained no air pockets as this would weaken the cannon which would then explode on firing. The Royal Cypher which appears on these guns is part of the casting process.

On completion of casting the cannon is bored out longitudinally and the vent hole reamed. The finished gun is proof tested by the manufacturer under the supervision of an officer from the Inspector General of the Ordnance and at this stage the sighting marks are applied by engraving. As private ships were also supplied by the gunfounders all Naval guns were engraved with the broad arrow.

Black Paint for Gun Barrels (Original Formula)

To one gallon of vinegar add a quarter pound of iron rust, let it stand for one week; then add a pound of dry lamp black and threequarters of a pound of copperas; stir it up at intervals for a couple of days.

Lay five to six coats on the gun with a sponge, allowing it to dry well between each application. Polish with linseed oil and soft woollen rag. It will look like ebony.

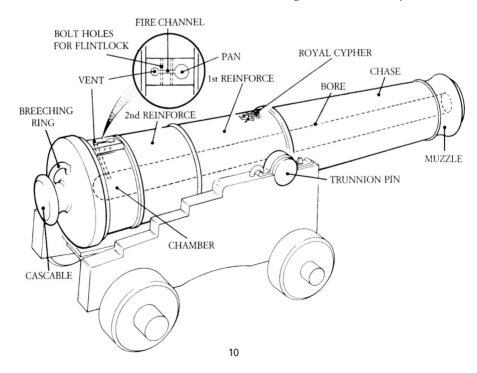

THE CARRONADE

The invention of the carronade is attributed to General Robert Melville and a Mr Gascoine. The date of the invention is 1779.

Carronades were the product of a factory on the River Carron at Falkirk, Scotland. Their first products were totally unreliable but within 2 years they had overcome the problems and obtained contracts with many merchant shipowners and the Navy. By 1781 there were over 400 ships armed with these guns which varied in size from 12lbs-68lbs. The following table shows the details of these guns:

Size	Bore	Length	Charge
12lbs	4.52in	32.36in	1lb
18lbs	5.16in	39.3in	1½lb
24lbs	5.68in	48.32in	2lb
68lbs	8.05in	83.75in	5½lb

The carronade was a major departure from the guns in service in this period. Those fitted in HMS Victory fired a 68lb ball using a charge of 5½lbs from a barrel of 7ft in length weighing 36cwts. By contrast the largest gun in the ship weighed 55cwts, had a barrel length of 10ft 3½ins and fired a 32lb ball using a charge of 10lbs. Just 5 men were required to service this gun compared to the 12 men required for the 32pdr.

When discussing the relative merits of the gun and the carronade comparison must be made of the use to which each was put. The cannon was a high velocity weapon ideal for fighting naval battles from a long range. When used at a close range the charge was almost invariably reduced to prevent the ball passing straight through the hull of the opposing vessel. The carronade on the other hand was a low velocity low charge short barrelled gun firing a large ball at close range. With low velocity the ball did not necessarily pass through the timber of the other ship but the action of striking caused massive splinters to be dislodged from the inside walls which whirled around the decks among the gun crews causing death, injury and havoc. No wonder this gun was called a "Devil Gun" or "Smasher".

The design of the carronade was unlike that of the cannon in that it incorporates many novel features.

The diameter of a normal round shot was such that it was a fairly loose fit in the bore. With the carronade the diameter of the round shot was much more accurately maintained in manufacture and fitted the bore better. The gap between the shot and the bore was known as "WINDAGE" and a gun had a better range and greater accuracy if the windage was as small as possible. Additionally the smaller the windage the less the charge needed to push it out of the barrel for the same range.

The carronade was also the first gun to be fitted with a DISPART sight. This sight enabled the gun captain to sight the weapon using the true bore line and thus achieve a more accurate shot at the target. The ability to aim the weapon was further improved by the fitting of an elevating screw to the rear of the gun and dispensing with the wooden wedge (coin/quoin).

The carronade carriage too was of a completely novel design. It was a simple block of timber (the bed) with a pair of trunnions at the front, a recoil pin and a plate to take the butt of the elevating screw.

The underside of the carronade was fitted with a lug instead of side trunnions and a pin passed through both trunnion brackets and the lug.

The sliding bed sat on a TRAINING BED which was fitted with a pivot pin fastened to a block of timber secured to the deck against the ships bulwarks. The rear of the training bed was supported on two iron trucks set at an angle which ran on a curved plate set into the deck. A longitudinal slot in the centre of the training bed received the recoil pin from the sliding bed and allows the carriage to recoil until brought up by the conventional breeching rope which ran through the breeching loop and side rings of the carriage.

When fired in the opening broadside at the stern of the French BUCENTAURE the carronade was loaded with a 5½lb charge, 68lb ball and a keg of 500 musket balls. This then was

Port and Starboard Carronades

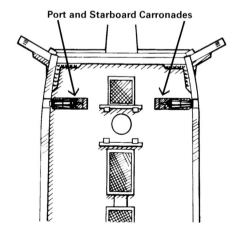

one of the principle advantages of the weapon, its ability to deliver a massive weight of shot in comparison with a cannon of the same weight and barrel length. The other advantage of the weapon was that very few men were required to man it.

One of the problems associated with the carronade was that senior naval officers decided that the superior fire power of the weapon rendered other weapons obsolete. Consequently they learnt their lesson the hard way. Ten years after the Battle of Trafalgar a British Squadron of 11 ships armed with carronades under Sir James YEO was badly battered by an American Squadron using 24 and 18 pounder cannon. Similarly a British ship HMS PHOEBE captured the American ship ESSEX by staying out of range using her cannon against the American carronades.

Where cannons and carronades were combined in the ships armament they became a potent force but on their own they were ineffective against cannon which could outrange them.

HMS Victory Figurehead

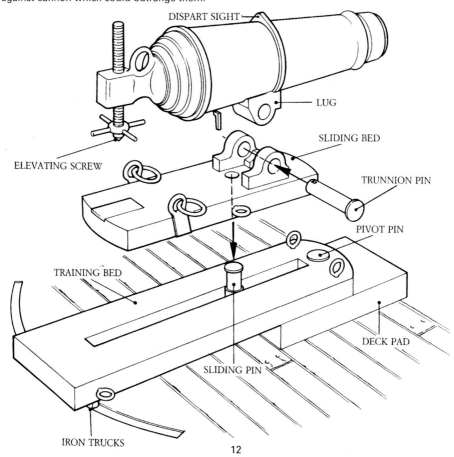

DISPART SIGHT

LUG

SLIDING BED

ELEVATING SCREW

TRUNNION PIN

PIVOT PIN

TRAINING BED

DECK PAD

SLIDING PIN

IRON TRUCKS

12

TYPES OF SHOT

A. Bar Shot: Solid cast iron shapes joined by a square or round bar. Used for cutting rigging, spars and sails.

B. Round Shot: Solid cast iron balls. Used to smash ship's sides and cause splintering and general damage. Splinters were the main cause of death either by maiming or infection of wounds. When firing at close quarters, guns were sometimes double or treble shotted. This caused maximum damage to the enemy but could be a danger to the ship's own crew. If the barrel was weak it could easily explode.

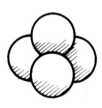

C. Chain Shot: Cast iron hemispheres joined by a chain. Used to cut rigging and spars.

D. Elongating Bar Shot: Thick circular plates joined by a sliding joint bar which could double in length during flight. Used to cut rigging, sails and spars.

E. Grape Shot: Round iron balls enclosed in a canvas bag, through the middle of which ran an iron spindle attached to an iron plate. Used mainly against personnel or against boarding party boats.

POWDER CHARGE

When sailors were punished and sentenced to be shackled in the punishment Bar, they were employed on various seamanship tasks, such as splicing, canvas work and oakum picking.

Other jobs which they were given would be sewing of cartridges and making of wads for the guns.

Cartridge bags were made of flannel (see note below) and supplied in a flat state. The dimensions of each size bag was also given in case supplies of ready cut bag were unavailable and they had to be manufactured on board. Each ship was supplied with cylindrical wooden formers for each type of gun and each weight of charge used. After the bag had been sewn into shape on the former it was filled with gun powder of the correct grain size. Strict instructions were in force to regulate the amount of powder used for each gun size and the type of charge to be made. The following list shows the sizes of charges required in HMS VICTORY.

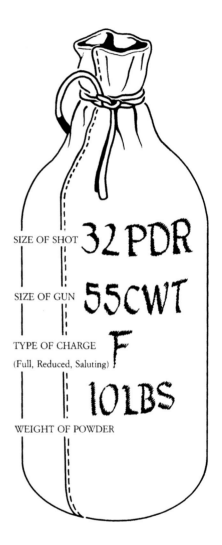

Gun	Full Charge	Reduced	Saluting
32lbs	10lbs	6lbs	6lbs
(14.4 kilos)	(4,5 kilos)		
24lbs	8lbs	4lbs	–
(11.0 kilos)	(3.5 kilos)		
12lbs	4lbs	–	–
(5.5 kilos)	(2.0 kilos)		

The finished size of a 32lb cartridge bag was approximately 6½ inches (16½cms) diameter and 8¼ inches (22cms) in length and the seams were sewn with worsted (wool). When loaded into the muzzle the seam was placed downwards so that it caused no resistance to the pricker which would enter the bag from the top through the vent.

Note: Some cartridges were made of flannel while others were made of paper (parchment) or a combination of flannel and paper. Some paper cartridges even had a wad loosely attached to the top so that ramming did not split the paper. In any event all cartridges had seams where the edges joined and these could obstruct the pricker.

ACCOUTREMENTS (Tools used at the guns)

A. Sponge: Sheepskin head on wooden stave. The head is approximately 12 inches long and the stave is about 11 feet long. In use the stave projected out of the gun port thus exposing the crew member to the fire of enemy musketeers.

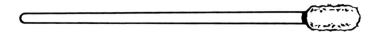

B. Rammer: Used to ram the shot, wad and cartridge down the bore. The head is flat to give a firm packing movement to the wad and cartridge. With the development of fuzed shell, the end of the rammer was made concaved with a recess to fit over the fuze. This is the type of rammer on display around the ship.

C. Worm: (Wadhook) A spiral double headed iron worm used to remove the wad and cartridge when unloading the gun. After 3 or 4 rounds, debris from the fired cartridges accumulated in the chamber and covered the bottom of the venthole thus preventing the flash penetrating to the cartridge. The worm was used to remove the debris.

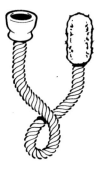

D. Flexible Rope Sponge and Rammer: Used in rough weather especially on the lower gun deck where the gun ports were only 4ft 6inches from the water line and the gun port remained closed until the gun was out and fired. When close alongside the enemy the rope sponge and rammer was used to prevent over exposure of the crew which could occur when using the long wooden stave with the gun port open.

Vent Reamer:
Square section iron spike with corkscrew twist at one end and handle at other used to clean vent hole of carbon debris.

Pricker:
Spike about 12 inches long used to prick the cartridge through the vent hole. This ensured that the cartridge was in the correct position in the bore and gave the flame from the firing pan easy access to the cartridge powder.

Match Tub:
Small wooden keg used to hold the slow match which was always kept burning at the rear of the gun in the event of flintlock failure.

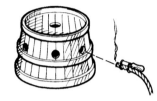

Shot Garland:
A circlet of rope used to contain one round shot at the rear of the gun. These garlands were superseded by racks of shot placed around the hatchways and coamings.

Salt Box:
A wooden box containing two cartridges placed at the rear of the gun. The Powder Monkey kept this box filled from the Hanging Magazine.

Handspikes:
Two handspikes were supplied to each gun. They were used to lift the rear of the gun to allow adjustment in sighting and to assist in training the gun so that it pointed out of the gun port at an angle and thus achieved a bearing advantage.

Match:
Length of cotton twisted in strands and made up into a rope. Soaked in saltpetre and vinegar and allowed to dry out it would smoulder for hours once ignited.

Vent Plug:
A tapered pin or palm glove which was forced into the vent after the gun fired. As the sponge was pushed into the bore the compression would extinguish any flames remaining. Without the plug, the air forced down the bore by the sponge would rush out the vent and make any debris burst into flames and thus delay the reloading cycle.

QUILL TUBES

Up to the middle of the 18th century the firing of cannon was achieved by pouring fine grain powder down the vent and into the channel and pan (see page 8). The powder was then ignited by the slow match and the gun fired.

Quill Tube Manufacture

Sir Charles DOUGLAS, a British Rear Admiral, is credited with the invention of the quill which greatly increased the rate of fire of British ships. Made from the feathers of the goose as these were of the right size and strength, a first rate ship of the line would carry over three thousand quills. If these were expended in action the gunner and his mates knew the method of manufacture and could make replacements.

(1) GOOSE QUILL

(3) END CUT WITH 7 BLADE CUTTER

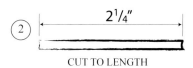

(2) 2¹/₄″ CUT TO LENGTH

(5) PAPER DISCS

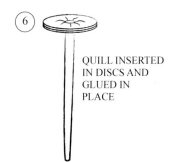

(4) CUT END BENT AT RIGHT ANGLES

(6) QUILL INSERTED IN DISCS AND GLUED IN PLACE

(7) TUBE FILLED WITH GROUND (MILLED) POWDER AND SPIRIT OF WINE PASTE

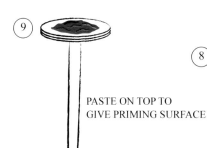

(9) PASTE ON TOP TO GIVE PRIMING SURFACE

(8) WIRE PASSED UP QUILL TO MAKE CENTRAL CHANNEL IN PASTE

THE MAGAZINES

There were six compartments in the ship which could be classified as magazines. A very large quantity of powder was required during a voyage and this was carried in the two main magazines. The largest or grand magazine was at the base of the foremast and the other at the base of the mizzen mast. Both these magazines had to be kept safe from enemy action so they were situated well down in the ship below the waterline, Gunpowder was supplied in casks about 3ft high and 1ft in diameter and these were stowed in barrel racks with retainer bars preventing their movement in a seaway.

Very detailed records were made of the expenditure of powder, shot, quills, etc., and these records were kept by the Gunner under the personal supervision of the Captain. The Gunners Log and Expenditure Book used in HMS VICTORY at the Battle of Trafalgar was held by Mr Rivers and is now in the Royal Naval Museum, Portsmouth, having been donated by Mrs Lily McCarthy.

Access to all magazines was through heavy locked doors, the keys of which were held by the Captain and only issued to the Gunner. This effectively prevented unauthorised persons tampering with the armament stores and causing mischief and damage to the ship.

When required for use, the powder was transferred one keg at a time from the main magazines to the two filling rooms. These rooms were adjacent to the magazines and contained all the equipment used to make up charges for the guns. Tools used by the gunners party were made from non-ferrous metal and as experience was gathered over the years, orders were issued that allowed all metal fittings, door hinges, locks, and even nails in the decks to be made of brass and copper. Felt slippers were issued for use in magazines and heavy material curtains-wetted continually - were hung at all the doors to brush granules of powder from the clothes and skin of the men as they passed through.

In 1800, orders were issued to the effect that all magazines were to be lined with copper sheet to prevent rats gnawing through the wood and

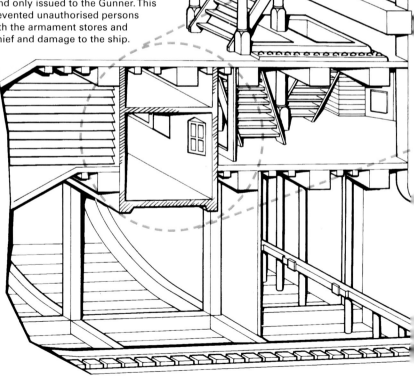

carrying powder back to their nests. On arrival in the filling room the cask was broached by the Gunner and gunners mates transferred the powder into the cartridge bags. Straight sided copper containers of various sizes were used to measure the powder as scales would not be effective at sea. When filled the bags were securely sealed ready for use, and transferred to the two hanging magazines.

Hanging magazines are secure boxes suspended between the Orlop deck and the Hold so that air could circulate all the way around and fire prevention methods put into operation. The top of the box was 3ft below the lower gun deck and the bottom of the box was 12ft above the keel. Access to these magazines was through a lobby protected by heavy doors guarded by a Marine sentry. To provide light in the magazine a lamp was placed in a small glass enclosed box which projected through the wall of the magazine but was only accessible from outside on the Orlop deck. This novel feature allowed normal working under all conditions without the risk of a naked flame igniting the powder.

The forward hanging magazine provided the cartridges for the lower and middle decks and the after magazine for the upper, fo'csle and quarterdecks. This avoided any confusion with the wrong size cartridge arriving at the wrong gun.

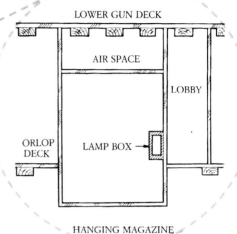

LOWER GUN DECK

AIR SPACE

LOBBY

ORLOP DECK

LAMP BOX →

HANGING MAGAZINE

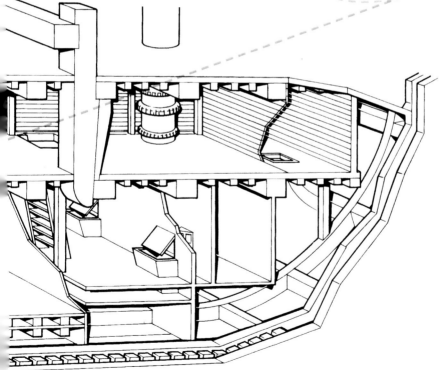

THE FLINTLOCK

The process of firing the gun by igniting a powder train caused a number of problems. The unpredictability of the train required an expert gunner to determine at which time to ignite so that the gun fired at the required instant. Delays in firing caused many misses when the ship was rolling in a seaway as the best position was with the ship upright and the guns horizontal. Secondly, the powder in the pan and fire channel could be blown away by a stiff breeze or the blast from the adjacent gun firing and a sustained rate of fire became impossible to achieve.

The introduction of the quill tube which dispensed with the powder train greatly increased the predictability of gunfire but

the major advance came with the invention of the flintlock. Flintlocks were being issued in 1746 but the resistance of ships captains to them meant delays in their use. Sir Charles Douglas had more faith in them and when fitted to his cannon achieved results which were so impressive that other Captains overcame their reluctance and following Douglas's drill achieved the same results. The flintlock has its own pan fire channel and the "frizzen" (priming pan cover) lowered into place protected the powder from blast. The flash hole in the pan was directly over the top of the quill so the delays in firing which had plagued the ship's gunners were eliminated. The diagram below shows flintlocks of 1922 manufacture and are for display only.

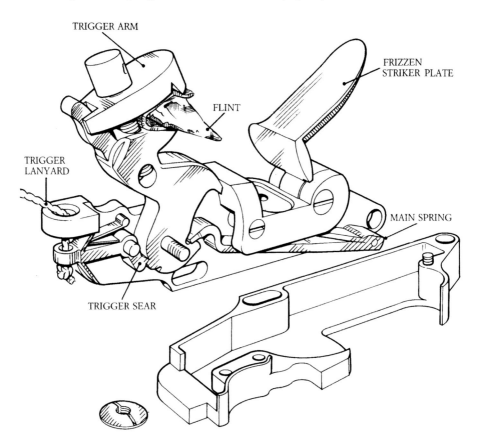

TRIGGER ARM

FRIZZEN
STRIKER PLATE

FLINT

TRIGGER
LANYARD

MAIN SPRING

TRIGGER SEAR

AMMUNITION SUPPLY

The allocation of manpower shows that 623 men were employed at the great guns and additionally over a hundred men and boys who took no actual part in the firing of the guns had jobs associated with the armament which were just as vital. A prudent captain would demand that a ready supply of powder and shot was available for any eventuality. When action was joined this ammunition was quickly expended and more would have to be prepared. This duty was carried out by 48 men in the grand, after and hanging magazines who had to work at a furious pace while still maintaining full safety precautions!

Having made up the charges they had to be transferred to the guns above and this was the task of the powder monkey who being young and agile could work his way from the hanging magazines to the hatchways which led to the deck above. There were three main hatchways through which ammunition was passed by the 19 men detailed for the task. At the fore hatch were 7 men, the main had 4 men and the after had 8 men. Some of these men operated a pulley system (called a whip) to hoist fresh supplies of shot to the upper decks from the shot lockers in the hold, and the others would pass the ammunition up to the men above by hand. As these hatchways were open a Marine sentry would be posted there to prevent men running away from their duties and hiding in the hold or Orlop.

GUN DRILL

Nelson had ensured that all his officers and guns crews were well trained and in comparison with our enemies (mainly the French and Spanish) our sailors managed a ratio of at least 4 to 1 in the action rate of fire. Some of our Captains were not as conscientious and the rate of fire was variable throughout the fleet. Our senior officers were tasked to ensure that our ships were not disadvantaged in battle and an order was issued to the Fleet (see appendix) to create a uniform system for the exercise of the Great Guns.

THE GUNS CREW

The number of men needed to man a gun depended on the size (and weight) of the gun. The table below shows the number of men on each deck, the number of guns and the number of men required for each gun.

Deck	No of Guns	Crew	No of Men per Deck
Quarterdeck	12 x 12pds	10	60
Upper Gun Deck	30 x 12 pds	10	150
Middle Gun Deck	28 x 24 pds	12	168
Lower Gun Deck	30 x 32 pds	15	225
Forecastle	2 x12 pds	10	–
Forecastle	2 x 68pds	10	20
	104		623

Each man had to know to which gun he was allocated so guns on each deck were given a number in sequence from the Bow to the Stern, ie. Port 1, 2, 3, 4, etc., and Starboard 1, 2, 3, 4, etc.. Traditionally ships formed parallel lines of battle so the Port side of one ship fought the Starboard side of the opposing ship. In this way each firing gun had a full crew. When attacked by ships on both sides a different method of manning the guns had to be arranged. Experience dictated that the best method was the crew of Port 1 would man Port 1 and 2, and the crew of Port 2 would man Starboard 1 and 2, Port 3 mans Port 3 and 4, and Port 4 would man Starboard 3 and 4. This continues all the way along each gun deck.

When preparing for action all guns would be loaded with powder and shot and at the order to fire the crew would fire their gun and proceed to the adjacent gun leaving two men behind whose duty is to start the re-loading cycle.

Each man was given a positional number at his gun and carried out his own tasks but by training he also learnt to perform the duties of all other men in the guns crew. Thus in the event of death or injury of the man who rams the shot into the barrel any other member of the crew could replace him and sustain the rate of fire.

In the case of a gun with a crew of 12 men the duties were allocated as follows:

No 1 and the Captain of the Gun	In charge of the gun and of aiming and firing.
No 2	Stops the vent, assists with the train tackles, fires the gun with match if flintlock not fitted.
No 3	Loads the cartridge and shot.
No 4	Uses the rammer to force the cartridge and shot down the bore. Uses sponge and worm to clean the bore.

THE GUNS CREW - continued

Nos 5, 6, 7and 8	Man the tackles fitted at the sides of the gun carriage.
Nos 9 and 10	Use handspikes to train the gun for aiming purposes.
No 11	Primes the gun.
No 12	Maintains the supply of ammunition to the gun.

THE POWDER MONKEY

Powder Monkeys were young men and boys who because of their agility could weave their way around the obstructions of the Orlop deck and any other deck on which they were employed during action. The scheme of complement or crew list is decided by the Admiralty Board and in the case of HMS VICTORY the number of boys was set at 40. Examination of the muster roll of the ship after the Battle of Trafalgar shows that 43 boys were on board on the 21 October 1805. The youngest boy was THOMAS TWITCHETT aged 12 years and the oldest boy was aged 20 years. These boys were not recruited by the press gangs which roamed the towns nor were they the inmates of the prisons. Some were the children of serving sailors who had no settled homes while others were supplied by the Marine Society.

The problems of waifs and strays had been recognised for a long time by the Magistrates of the big cities. Jonas Hanway (1712-1786) a philanthropist, convinced the magistrates that with his plan to found the Marine Society he would undertake to educate and find useful employment at sea for the waifs and strays of London. Naval Captains welcomed the idea as it eased the problems of recruitment and thus reduced the need for pressed men.

PREPARE FOR ACTION

When sailors joined a ship they were allocated to either the Larboard (Port) or Starboard watch. This effectively divided the ship's company into two parts and ensured that there were sufficient sailors to run the ship day and night and allow rest, relaxation and training. Those sailors who were detailed as gun crews were further sub-divided into groups showing which deck and which gun they were to man during fighting. The command structure for each deck was as follows:

Deck	Officers	Mates	Midshipmen
Forecastle	Boatswain	1	1
Upper Gun Deck	2 Lieutenants	1	4
Middle Gun Deck	2 Lieutenants	1	5
Lower Gun Deck	2 Lieutenants	1	5
Quarterdeck	1 Lieutenant	–	2

In todays modern navy the expression used to call all men from their daily jobs to man the armament, sonar and radio equipment when threatened by an enemy is 'ACTION STATIONS'. At the time of Trafalgar the drummer would be called upon to take his drum and 'BEAT TO QUARTERS'.

Many hours of practice went into training the ship's company to make the preparations which would transform the ship from a peaceful sailing vessel into a deadly war machine. When you look around HMS VICTORY you will see hammocks hanging from their hooks, mess tables and benches between the guns, partitions, tables and chairs in the Great Cabin and boats on the skid beams. At the sound of the drum all hands ran to their duties.

Everyman knew what he had to do and the work involved wetting and sanding the decks, taking down the partitions, stowing all the mess tables and officers furniture in the hold, rigging wet curtains over the magazine doors, providing hoses from the pumps, wetting the sails to minimise fire risk and to enable them to hold air better, lowering the boats over the side and towing them astern and of course, preparing the guns for action.

BEAT TO QUARTERS (Enemy in Sight)

As the beat of the drum reached the lower reaches of the ship the ship's company hurried to clear the ship for action and prepare the guns for firing. Exercises and drills enabled a ship the size of HMS VICTORY to clear for action in under 10 minutes. This represents a sailing distance of about 1 mile so a ship would be fully prepared for at least half an hour before action was joined. Whilst the majority of the gun crews mustered at their guns, the powder man would proceed to the magazines to collect two cartridges in a salt box. Thereafter he will only collect one at a time and the powder monkeys will supply the remainder.

On arrival at the gun, the gun captain will order each man to call out his positional number. When each man has responded the gun captain will order:

"Clear for Action"
After the last firing or practice, the gunport lid was hauled taut into the gun port and, especially on the Lower Gun Deck, the gaps may even have been stuffed with rag or old rope to make it water tight.

The coin (quoin) would have been removed from under the breech and the muzzle then elevated to its maximum. The gun was then run in to the ship's side and the side tackles secured. The muzzle was lashed to the rings above the gun port and the train tackle removed and stowed. In this position the gun could remain for days, being checked occasionally to make sure it was secure. The first action of the crew, therefore was to remove the muzzle lashings and rig the side and train tackles. Other members of the guns crew would ensure that the match and match tub, rammer, sponge, worm, handspikes, quills, priming powder, vent plugs, vent reamer and all other accessories were provided.

"Cast Loose the Gun"
The gun port is pushed open with the butt end of the rammer by No 3 while 5, 6, 7 and 8 haul in the overhead tackle to raise the gunport lid. When high enough the tackle is turned up on the cleat. The tampion which sealed the muzzle is now removed by No 4.

"Load"
No 3 receives his cartridge from No 12 and enters it into the gun so that the seam is downward. (If paper and flannel - the flannel end first, if all flannel then the sewn end first). No 4 now uses the rammer to push the cartridge to the bottom of the bore. When home he gives it two sharp blows with the rammer. As the gun is going to be used immediately

there is no need for No 3 to place a wad between the charge and the shot, but a wad is always to be put in after the shot and both rammed home together. When home, No 4 is to give three sharp blows with the rammer, place the rammer on the deck and with No 3 return to their proper places on the side tackles.

"Run out the Gun"
The crew take up the slack in the side tackles and haul the gun towards the side of the ship while the gun captain allows the train tackle to overhaul itself and simultaneously ensures that the breeching rope passing through the side rings on the carriage does not get caught under the trucks. The breeching is then laid on top of the carriage.

"Prick the Cartridge"
Crew member 11 takes the pricker from his belt and placing it in the vent hole forces it down into the cartridge. When he withdraws it he examines the point to ascertain whether it entered the cartridge. If there is no trace of powder he repeats the operation and if still unsuccessful he makes a report to the Gun Captain who orders the cartridge to be rammed again.

"Prime"
No 11 carries two pouches on his belt. From one he takes a quill tube and places it in the vent and from the other he takes a priming cartridge and sprinkles powder into the gun channel and the flintlock pan.

"Point"
All crew members take up the side tackles and hand spikes and await the directions of the gun captain. By hauling on the right hand tackle and using the left handspike the barrel is pointed to the left and vice-versa. When satisfied with the direction of the gun the gun captain must consider what elevation he requires.

Before the days of the quartersights the gun captain had to rely on experience and used the guide shown on page 28. Crew members 9 and 10 inserted their handspikes under the breech of the gun and acting on the gun captain's orders raise or lower the breech while the gun captain adjusts the position of the coin (quoin). When satisfied the gun captain orders:

"Make Ready"
The gun captain cocks the flintlock and lowers the frizzen into position before retiring to the full extent of the trigger lanyard. He looks carefully along his sights and at the appropriate time orders:

"Fire"

Gun captains are responsible and experienced men who are trusted to use their own initiative. Waiting for the moment that allowing for the ships movement and the delay in the firing cycle when he judges he will hit the target, he pulls the lanyard.

Two and a half tons of weapon thunders back across the deck until brought up by the breeching rope. No 12 who had been holding the fall of the train tackle now rapidly hauls away until the slack is gone and then takes a turn to hold the gun in the "Run In" position. As the gun recoiled crewman No 2 forced a vent plug into the vent to stop the gases escaping and thus causing a build up of carbon in the vent hole. In non-firing practices the insertion of the vent plug would have been ordered by the command "STOP THE TOUCHOLE". The gun captain now orders:

"Sponge"

No 4 takes the sponge from No 6 and forces it into the gun with one steady push until it is home. He then rotates the sponge three times before withdrawing it from the barrel. The gun captain now orders:

"Load"

The sequence continues until "CEASE FIRE" and "SECURE THE GUNS". The powder man returns the unused powder to the magazine whilst all other crew members secure the gun and return the equipment to its proper stowages.

Worming the Gun

Continual firing of the gun caused a build up of cartridge bag residue in the chamber of the gun. If this was not removed it would eventually block the bottom of the vent and prevent the gun being fired. To overcome this, the Admiralty Board decreed that after 4 rounds had been fired the worm must be used to remove the residue. The order "WORM THE GUN" would be given after the order "SPONGE" in the drill sequence.

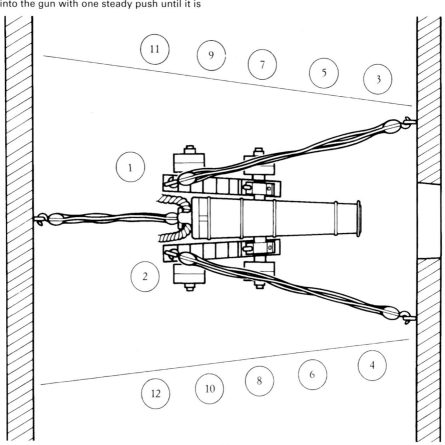

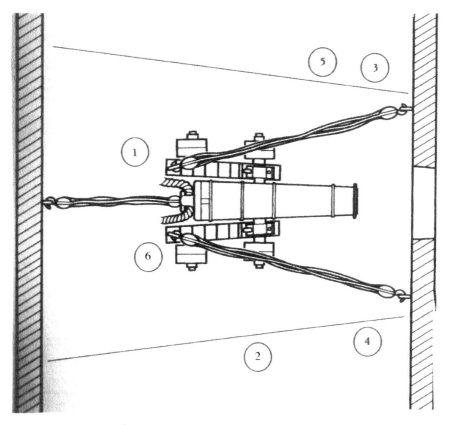

4, Sponges, &c.

3, Loads, &c.

3 , 4 , 5 , 2 , 1 Run the gun out.

3,4, Attend the quarter-tackle.

5,2, Attend the handspikes, and 5 gives cartridge, shot, and wad, to 3.

6, Keeps the cartridge-box supplied.

2, The Second Captain, stops the vent, &c.

1, The Captain, primes, points, and commands, &c., and attends to the train-tackle.

SIGHTING THE GUN

When the cannon is being bored the muzzle and centre of the breech are marked with engraved lines. The lines on the top of the breech and muzzle are classified as the 'Line of Metal' (LM). The lines on either side of the muzzle and breech are on the 'Centre of the Metal' (CM).

When the barrel is mounted in the carriage it is held in place by hinged brackets called "capsquares" which fit over the trunnions. These capsquares effectively prevent the breech and muzzle centre of metal notches being aligned for sighting purposes. To overcome this problem further notches (Q) are engraved slightly above the centre of metal notches on both the muzzle and breech.

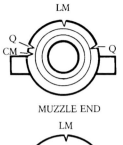

MUZZLE END

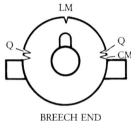

BREECH END

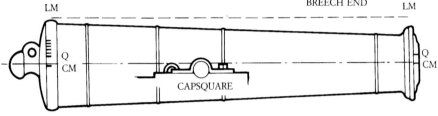

CAPSQUARE

The breech notch is also the basis of the strip of engraved numbered notches. These 13 notches mark divisions representing quarters of degree from 0 to 3 degrees. These are called "quarter sights" and were introduced long after the Battle of Trafalgar.

To demonstrate this feature a portable piece of iron known as the DISPART sight is fitted on a flat portion on top of the piece just above the trunnions.

The gun captain uses the breech LM and Dispart sight to lay the gun horizontal and thus demonstrate the correction factor when laying the gun on the target.

As the barrel is tapered, lining up the notches LM-LM on top of the piece will give the correct direction to the shot but will also give an elevation to the gun which could cause the shot to go over the target.

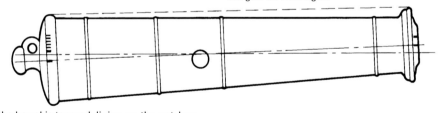

DISPART

Elevation for Range

It was Nelson's policy that gunfire was to be aimed to cause damage to the hull and he did not care for the idea of firing at the masts to cause damage prior to boarding. To judge the elevation to achieve the range, the gun captain used the aiming marks.

The coin (or quoin) which supports the breech is also marked with notches which represent degrees of elevation so the angle can be found by trial and error and then all guns set to the same notch.

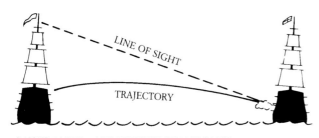

RANGE 1 MILE – AIM AT TRUCK OF MAINMAST

RANGE ½ MILE – AIM AT FIGHTING TOP

RANGE 400 YARDS – POINT BLANK

TACTICS

Tactics have been evolving since the very early days of sail. The introduction of steam gave rise to the introduction of many more but still the basic tactics used by Nelson's Navy remained unchanged. If a captain in those days took his ship into action and was badly beaten he would have to face a court martial to explain the defeat and one of the first questions he would have to answer was 'Did you have the weather gauge?'

Weather Gauge

Having the weather gauge meant being to windward of the enemy. Figure shows two ships closing to do battle. The ship on the left has the weather gauge.

The advantages of the weather gauge were:

a. Better manoeuvrability

b. Clear view of enemy unhindered by smoke

c. Facility to take the enemy's stern if she turns.

The advantages of the Lee gauge were:

a. Facility to keep lower gun ports open in strong wind and high sea

b. The men on the upper deck of the ship to windward were exposed to grape and musket shot.

WIND ⟶

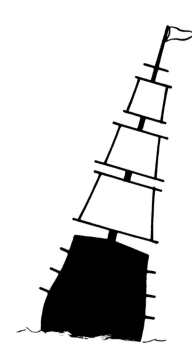

WEATHER LEE

THE BATTLE OF TRAFALGAR

At the Battle of Trafalgar Nelson split his fleet into two groups which approached the French fleet at right angles. As a result the French Admiral Villeneuve ordered his port guns to fire on the approaching English fleet and to close the gaps on his own line. Nelson, however, had briefed all his captains that he would search for gaps in the enemy line so that he could pass through them and engage them on their unprepared lee side. What Nelson intended was a brilliant strategy because he had a further weapon, which used correctly could dramatically affect the course of the battle. With his intentions known to the crews

he prepared both sides of the ship for action but ensured that the port side was the primary side.

As HMS VICTORY passed through the French line under the stern of the French Flagship BUCENTAURE she fired every gun on the port side through the stern windows of the French ship.

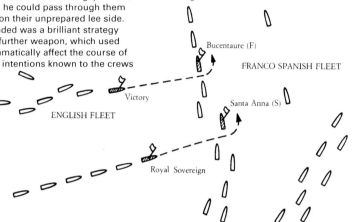

HMS VICTORY - CASUALTIES

During the Battle of Trafalgar 57 men were killed and 102 were wounded.

Royal Navy killed		Landsmen	6
Admiral	1	Boys	3
Commissioned Officer	1	Royal Marines killed	
Midshipmen	2	Officer	1
Petty Officers	3	NCO	1
Supply, Supernumeries & Retinue	2	Privates	15
Able Seamen	9	Drummer	1
Ordinary Seamen	12		

SHOT & POWDER EXPENDED AT TRAFALGAR

Item	32pdr	24pdr	12pdr
Cartridges	937	1234	1799
Round shot	997	872	800
Double headed	10	11	14
Grape shot	10	20	156

17190 pounds (7735 kilos) of gunpowder was used to fire 62432 lbs (28094 kilos) of shot, some 2669 rounds. This is 7.6 tons of gunpowder to fire 28 tons of shot. Fully loaded VICTORY carried 120 tons of shot and 35 tons of powder.

The last of VICTORY's Trafalgar ratings was Seaman James Chapman, he died in 1876 aged 91 at Dundee.

The French Admiral at Trafalgar, Admiral Villeneuve, was taken prisoner. At his request, he was allowed to attend Nelsons funeral at St Pauls. January 9th 1806. When released, he returned to France, where he committed suicide by stabbing himself 6 times......???

SHORE BATTERIES

Over the centuries the British, French, and Spanish fought continual battles for possession of the Islands of the West Indies. Each nation in turn landed sailors and soldiers to capture islands and establish bases for their countries, Once captured the islands had to be fortified and for this the ships landed some of their own cannon.

Although the large ship's boats were capable of taking the weight of the heaviest gun, there were no landing stages or cranes to hoist them out, nor could the boats pass through the surf in an unstable condition with the additional top weight. To overcome this problem the guns were slung underneath' the boats and towed ashore to the beaches. Across the thwarts of the boat were placed two stout pieces of timber and around these timbers were hung two large rope slings. It is from these slings that the gun was suspended and transferred. Cannon selected for transfer are brought to the nearest hatchway and hoisted up and over the ships side by tackles suspended from the lower yards. As the gun is lowered over the side the weight is transferred to the slings under the boat.

As the boat reaches the beach the cannon will ground and can be dragged clear of the water.

Once the cannon were landed, there was concern over the effectiveness and fighting ability of the ship. Any enemy faced by a ship - even a larger one - which had empty gun ports would immediately be encouraged to fight and would eventually win. To overcome this problem a dummy gun barrel was set into the gun port in place of the displaced cannon and to all intents and purposes the ship had the appearance of being fully armed. This dummy gun was named a "QUAKER" and so called because the potential enemy would 'quake' at the sight of the 'fully armed' ship.

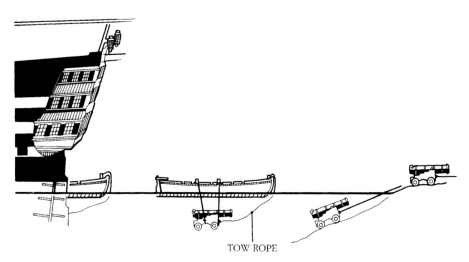

TOW ROPE

BENEFITS OF PRACTICE

As an island nation Great Britain relies on maritime trade for her existence. For centuries the Navy has been guardian of our shores and as a result has been continually seeking to destroy the ships of other nations which threaten us. Battle honours with strange sounding names abound in the history of the Royal Navy and although our enemies have been from all parts of the world it is the Spanish and French who posed the greatest threat. At almost every fleet action the British were victorious and morale was always at a peak. The British sailor believed he was invincible and that everything British was the best. In the years leading up to Trafalgar the British had defeated the Spanish at St Vincent, the French at the Nile and the Danes at Copenhagen.

When Napoleon considered the time was right he intended to cross the channel and invade England. To this end he wanted to remove or destroy the Channel Fleet. For years he had concentrated his efforts in developing his armies and neglected his navy and the British knew that so long as Napoleon's fleet was blockaded in his ports then England was safe from invasion. Thus it was that the British seaman was constantly on the high seas practising his skills and excercising his guns. The French and Spanish remained in harbour unable to venture forth. The net result was that the English could load, fire and reload a 32 pdr in 90 seconds, whereas the French and Spanish required 5 minutes for the same operation. It was these factors, plus the leadership and the dedication of the men which were instrumental in the Royal Navy holding the supreme position against the navies in the rest of the world for many years.

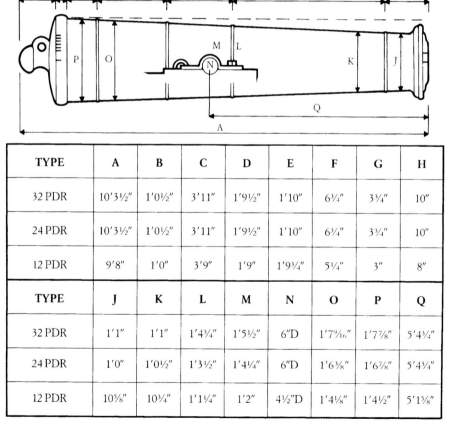

TYPE	A	B	C	D	E	F	G	H
32 PDR	10'3½"	1'0½"	3'11"	1'9½"	1'10"	6¾"	3¾"	10"
24 PDR	10'3½"	1'0½"	3'11"	1'9½"	1'10"	6¾"	3¾"	10"
12 PDR	9'8"	1'0"	3'9"	1'9"	1'9¾"	5¼"	3"	8"

TYPE	J	K	L	M	N	O	P	Q
32 PDR	1'1"	1'1"	1'4¾"	1'5½"	6"D	1'7⁹⁄₁₆"	1'7⅞"	5'4¾"
24 PDR	1'0"	1'0½"	1'3½"	1'4¼"	6"D	1'6⅜"	1'6⅞"	5'4¾"
12 PDR	10⅝"	10¾"	1'1¼"	1'2"	4½"D	1'4⅛"	1'4½"	5'1⅝"

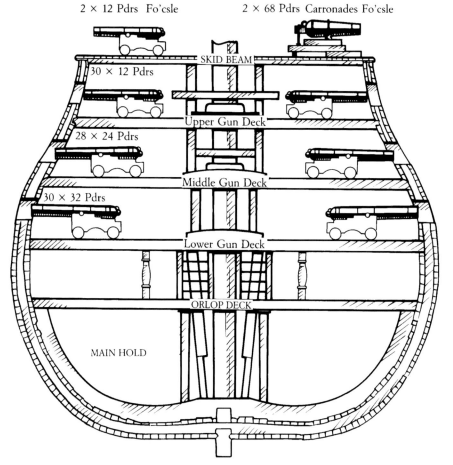

12 × 12 Pdrs   Quarterdeck

2 × 12 Pdrs Fo'csle   2 × 68 Pdrs Carronades Fo'csle

SKID BEAM

30 × 12 Pdrs

Upper Gun Deck

28 × 24 Pdrs

Middle Gun Deck

30 × 32 Pdrs

Lower Gun Deck

ORLOP DECK

MAIN HOLD

THE CREW OF HMS VICTORY

Including Admiral Lord Nelson, there were 821 on board VICTORY at Trafalgar
comprising:

Commissioned Officers	9
Non Commissioned Officers & Warrant Officers	16
Midshipmen	21
Petty Officers	61
Supply, Supernumeries & Admirals retinue	43
Able Seamen	212
Ordinary Seamen	193
Landsmen	87
Boys	31
Royal Marines under Captain Adair	146
Lieutenants	3
Non-Commissioned Officers	7
Privates	132
Drummers	3
Trumpeter	1

Many different nationalities were on board VICTORY at Trafalgar
including:

Africans	1		Indians	2
Americans	22		Jamaican	1
Brazilian	1		Maltese	6
Canadians	2		Norwegian	2
Dutch	2		Portuguese	1
Danes	7		Swedes	4
French	4		Swiss	2
Germans	2		West Indian	4

Appendix

By the Commissioners for executing the Office of Lord High Admiral of the United Kingdom of Great Britain and Ireland, &c. &c.

WHEREAS We think it highly expedient that an uniform system for the exercise of the Great Guns of His Majesty's Ships should be established, so that the Officers and Men belonging to one Ship may be capable of co-operating immediately with the Crew of another, and the Royal Marines, and Royal Marine Artillery, may be equally fit to assist in fighting any Ship on board which they may from time to time be employed; We have directed the annexed Instructions for the Exercise of the Great Guns to be prepared; and We do hereby require and direct that, from this date, the Exercise, as in these Instructions set forth, and *no other*, shall be used and practised on board all His Majesty's Ships and Vessels of War, and by the Royal Marines and Royal Marine Artillery ashore and afloat; and We do strictly enjoin all Commanders in Chief, and Commandants of Royal Marines respectively, that they take care that the said Exercise be immediately introduced into all Ships and Vessels, and the respective Divisions of Royal Marines under their command ; and that they see that the Captains, Commanders, and all other Officers, do carefully and diligently attend to the training of their respective Ships' Companies, or Divisions or Companies of Royal Marines, to the said Exercise, and to all the parts and details thereof, without any deviation or exception whatsoever ; and all Commanders in Chief shall, from time to time, and as often as they shall see necessary, go on board the several Ships and Vessels under their Orders, and shall see their Crews Exercised before them, according to the said Exercise, in all the different modes and circumstances mentioned in the said Instructions ; and all the Commandants of the several Divisions of Royal Marines, and Royal Marine Artillery, shall see the same duty practised by the Officers and Men under their orders.

And whereas We consider the uniformity,

celerity, and precision of the **Great Guns** to be vitally important to the **honour** of His Majesty's Arms and to the **safety** of the Country, We do most strictly **and** earnestly command and enjoin all **Officers to** pay, according to their several **ranks, the** greatest attention to this subject, and **to spare** no exertion in training the **Seamen and** Royal Marines to an uniform, **quick and** precise practice of the Great Guns **agreeably** to the said Instructions.

Given under our Hands the **1st of** *August* 1817.

> **MELVILLE.**
> **GEO. HOPE.**
> **G. MOORE.**

*By Command of their **Lordships**,*

> **J. W. CROKER**

The respective Flag Officers, Captains, Commanders, and Officers commanding His Majesty's Ships and Vessels, and to the several Officers commanding the Royal Marines.

Extracted from "Instructions for the Exercise of the Great Guns" published by John Murray dated 1824.